Prayer Journal

A Journey of Prayer, Praise
and Gratitude

BLESS THE LORD O MY SOUL

PSALM 103:1

Many only recognize their
need for God when things begin
to fall apart.
However, God's desire is
for us to pray
"on all occasions with all kinds
of prayers and requests"

~ Ephesians 6:18

Prayers for My Family

DATE	NAME

Be Still and Know That I'm With You...

Psalm 46:10

Prayers for Myself

DATE	REFLECTIONS

Prayers For My Friends

DATE	NAMES

For with God, nothing is impossible...

DATE	NAMES

Prayers For My Loves

DATE	NAME	

My Prayer

Prayer Journal

DATE / /

Spiritual Inspiration

" I can do All THINGS through CHRIST WHO STRENGTHENS ME "

- PHILIPPIANS 4:13 -

Sermon Journal

DATE   /   /

WHAT I LEARNED TODAY

Notes:

" The GOD of my ROCK in Him will I TRUST "

- 2 SAMUEL 22:3 -

Lord Teach Me To

I Am Grateful For

Prayer Requests

Sermon Journal

DATE / /

Notes:

" I will walk by
FAITH
even when I can't
SEE "

- 2 CORINTHIANS 5:1 -

Lord Teach Me To

I Am Grateful For

Prayer Requests

Sermon Journal

WHAT I LEARNED TODAY

Notes:

" Be Still
in the Presence
of the LORD
and wait patiently
for him to act. "

- PSALM 37:7 -

Lord Teach Me To

I Am Grateful For

Prayer Requests

Sermon Journal

DATE / /

WHAT I LEARNED TODAY

Notes:

" I Praise You
I AM BECAUSE
fearfully and wonderfully
MADE"

- PSALM 134:14 -

Lord Teach Me To

I Am Grateful For

Prayer Requests

Sermon Journal

DATE / /

WHAT I LEARNED TODAY

Notes:

"*Be Not Afraid,* ONLY **BELIEVE**"

- MARK 5:36 -

I AM GRATEFUL FOR

Lord Teach Me To

I Am Grateful For

Prayer Requests

Sermon Journal

DATE / /

WHAT I LEARNED TODAY

Notes:

" *By his wounds*
WE ARE **HEALED** "

- ISAIAH 53:5 -

I AM GRATEFUL FOR

Prayer Requests

DATE	NAMES

Prayer Card

Prayer Card

Hymn Study

HYMN:

Favorite Verse

Lyrics of Faith

Sing to him, Sing praise to him, tell of all his wonderful acts.

Psalm 105:2

Sermon Notes

DATE / / **TOPIC:**

SPEAKER:　　　　　　　　　**PLACE OF WORSHIP:**

SCRIPTURE

NOTES

Key Points

Sermon Tracker

SCRIPTURE

NOTES

Reflections

Today's stand-out verse:

I am thankful for:

Prayer Requests:

Inspirational Scripture:

Sermon Notes

DATE / / **TOPIC**

Scripture

Prayer & Praise

Personal Reflections

Sermon Tracker

DATE

SCRIPTURE

NOTES

Reflections

Today's stand-out verse:

I am thankful for:

Prayer Requests:

Inspirational Scripture:

Sermon Notes

DATE / /

SERMON

Scripture

Notes

Be on your guard; stand firm in the faith; be courageous; be strong.

1 Corinthians 4:16-18

Sermon Tracker

SCRIPTURE

NOTES

Reflections

DATE

Today's stand-out verse: I am thankful for:

Prayer Requests: Inspirational Scripture:

Sermon Notes

SPEAKER: PLACE OF WORSHIP:

Key Points

In God We Trust

This week I will focus on:

What I am most grateful for:

In God We Trust

This week I was most blessed by:

My calling in life is:

In God We Trust

My favorite passage of scripture is:

God is leading me to make the following changes:

In God We Trust

I feel God's presence most when:

What brings me the most joy is:

In God We Trust

My spiritual gifts are:

My enthusiasm for the gospel is increased when:

In God We Trust

One way I can apply the gospel to my life is:

An act of obedience God is prompting me to take is:

My Time With The Lord

Scripture that inspired me today:

Dear Lord:

Lord Teach Me To

I Am Grateful For

Prayer Requests

"Not by My STRENGTH, by His"

-Zechariah 4:6-

Lord Teach Me To

I Am Grateful For

Prayer Requests

" Be Still
in the Presence
of the LORD
and wait patiently "
for him to act.
- PSALM 37:7 -

Lord Teach Me To

I Am Grateful For

Prayer Requests

"I will not be
SHAKEN "
- PSALM 16:8 -

Lord Teach Me To

I Am Grateful For

Prayer Requests

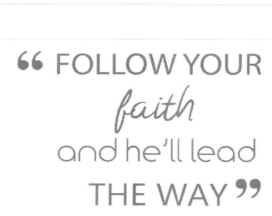

" FOLLOW YOUR *faith* **and he'll lead THE WAY "**

Lord Teach Me To

I Am Grateful For

Prayer Requests

Lord Teach Me To

I Am Grateful For

Prayer Requests

My Time With The Lord

Scripture that inspired me today:

Dear Lord:

Lord Teach Me To

I Am Grateful For

Prayer Requests

My Time With The Lord

Scripture that inspired me today:

Dear Lord:

Lord Teach Me To

I Am Grateful For

Prayer Requests

My Time With The Lord

DATE:

Scripture that inspired me today:

Dear Lord:

Lord Teach Me To

I Am Grateful For

Prayer Requests

My Time With The Lord

DATE:

Scripture that inspired me today:

Dear Lord:

Lord Teach Me To

I Am Grateful For

Prayer Requests

My Time With The Lord

Scripture that inspired me today:

Dear Lord:

Lord Teach Me To

I Am Grateful For

Prayer Requests

My Time With The Lord

Scripture that inspired me today:

Dear Lord:

Lord Teach Me To

I Am Grateful For

Prayer Requests

Made in the USA
Las Vegas, NV
21 November 2021

34955615R00068